Reading Essentials
in Science

THE HUMAN BODY

The Digestive System

SUSAN GLASS

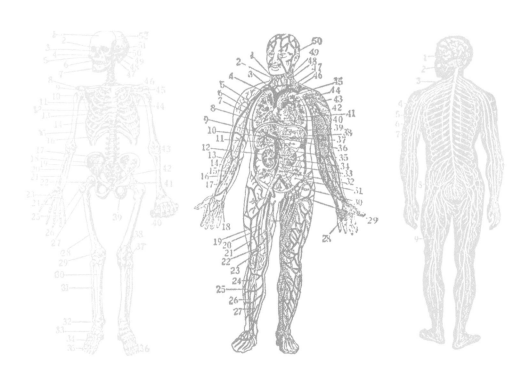

PERFECTION LEARNING®

Editorial Director:	Susan C. Thies
Editor:	Mary L. Bush
Design Director:	Randy Messer
Book Design:	Brianne Osborn
	Emily J. Greazel
Cover Design:	Michael A. Aspengren

A special thanks to the following for their scientific review of the book:

Paul Pistek, Instructor of Biological Sciences, North Iowa Area Community College

Jeffrey Bush, Field Engineer, Vessco, Inc.

Image Credits:

© Mark Garten/CORBIS: cover (bottom left), p. 10; © Norbert Schaefer/CORBIS: p. 11 (top)

ClipArt.com: pp. 1, 3, 4 (background), 8 (background), 9, 12 (background), 20, 22 (background), 25 (background), 26, 32 (bottom), 34 (background), 41 (left), 42, 46 (background), 47 (background), 48 (background); Corel Professional Photos: pp. 28, 39; Dynamic Graphics: pp. 5, 31 (top), 33, 41 (right), 43 (left); LifeART © 2003 Lippincott, Williams, & Wilkins: cover (bottom right), pp. 7, 12 (bottom), 13, 14, 17, 18, 19, 21, 23 (top), 24; Perfection Learning Corporation: pp. 11 (bottom), 35, 37, 38 (bottom); Photos.com: cover (background), cover (bottom center), back cover, pp. 4 (bottom), 15, 16, 27, 29, 30, 31 (bottom), 32 (top), 36, 38 (top), 40, 43 (right), 45; © Royalty-Free/CORBIS: pp. 6, 23 (bottom)

Perfection Learning® Corporation
1000 North Second Avenue, P.O. Box 500
Logan, Iowa 51546-0500.
Phone: 1-800-831-4190
Fax: 1-800-543-2745
perfectionlearning.com

1 2 3 4 5 6 BA 08 07 06 05 04 03
ISBN 0-7891-6029-3

Contents

Introduction

Are you hungry? Did you know that the average person eats about three pounds of food a day? That's about 1000 pounds a year and more than 30 tons in a lifetime! Where does all that food go? You digest it!

Digest comes from a word that means "to divide." To divide means to break up into smaller pieces. One of the jobs of your digestive system is to break food down into tiny pieces that your body can use. Another job is to get the pieces of broken-down food into your blood so your body can use them for energy.

When you digest a piece of food, it doesn't stand a chance. It gets bitten, chewed, mashed, and attacked by **chemicals**.

It is mercilessly broken down into pieces so small they pass right through your **intestinal** wall into your **bloodstream**. Digestion breaks down your food physically (smashing, tearing, mashing, squeezing) and chemically (changing from one substance to another).

Your digestive system absorbs all the usable parts of the food you eat. These are called *nutrients*. Nutrients from food keep you healthy and alive. Once the nutrients are in your blood, your **circulatory system** can carry them to your **cells**. Your body parts are made up of trillions of these tiny cells. Each cell needs food to stay alive and do its job. Nutrients also provide energy so you can think, move, and grow. They even supply the materials your body needs to repair itself.

After the digestive system has removed the nutrients from food, it pushes the leftovers that it can't use out of your body. This useless stuff gets flushed down the toilet without so much as a thank-you or good-bye.

Life as a French Fry

Imagine that you are a french fry. You have just been eaten by a hungry teenager. When you get past those slicing teeth and the sloshing in saliva, you begin the scary slide down the esophagus. After the mashing and the acid bath in the stomach, you are definitely not your old self anymore. Then you begin a terrifying trip through two long, dark tubes where you are squeezed and attacked by burning chemicals. Anyone meeting up with you in the dark, wet, **mucus**-lined alleyways of the digestive system wouldn't recognize you at all.

By the end of your long journey through the intestines, the transformation is complete. You have been separated into pieces that no longer look like the fry you once were. Some of those pieces are swept away in the bloodstream and scattered throughout the body. The rest gets pushed outside and flushed away.

Meet the Digestive System

Your digestive system includes a long tube called the *alimentary canal*, which begins at your mouth and ends at your anus. The mouth, pharynx, esophagus, stomach, intestines, and rectum are all part of the alimentary canal. Your liver, gallbladder, and pancreas are also parts of the digestive system. These **organs** contribute juices that help digest food.

Working together, the parts of your digestive system break down food, pull out nutrients your body needs, and get rid of waste. Imagine how much work your digestive system has to do to digest the 30 tons of food you'll eat in your lifetime!

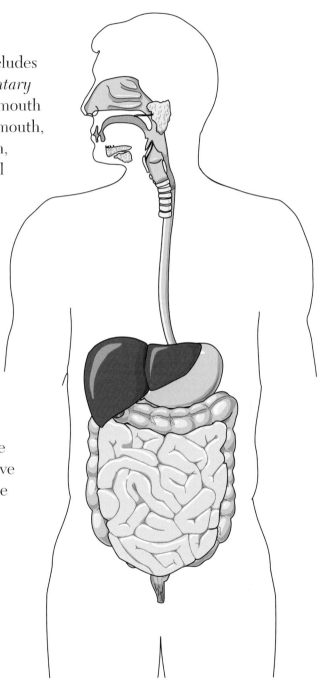

CHAPTER

1

It All Begins in the Mouth

The digestion process begins when you put food into your mouth. Whether you eat a potato chip, an apple, or a ham sandwich, the journey starts when you open wide and stuff food inside.

Terrifying Teeth

The next time you chew on something, think about your teeth. You bite or tear food with your front teeth called *incisors*. Incisors cut and nip. They are flat and wedge-shaped—perfect for cutting.

Now feel the pointy teeth on either side of the incisors. These are called canine teeth. *Canine* means "dog." Your canines are pointed just like a dog's teeth. Canines help to grab hold of food and tear it.

To the sides of your canines are the bicuspids. The name *bicuspid* means "having two points." If you feel these teeth with your tongue, you will understand how they got that name. Bicuspids are used to crush and mash food.

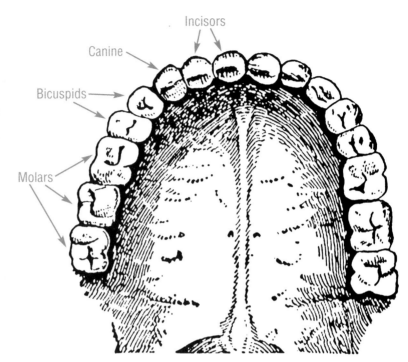

Behind the bicuspids are your back teeth, or molars. *Molar* comes from a word meaning "millstones." Millstones were large stones used for grinding wheat and other grains into flour. Your molars are grinders. They smash up your food.

Chew on This!

Children have 20 teeth in their first set of teeth. Adults normally have 32 permanent teeth.

Animals that eat meat are carnivores. Picture the teeth of meat-eating lions, dogs, or sharks. They have pointed teeth for ripping and tearing meat.

Animals that eat plants are herbivores. Plant eaters, like cows and sheep, have mostly flat teeth for nipping and grinding up grasses and leaves.

Animals that eat both plants and meat are called *omnivores*. Omnivores have both pointy and flat teeth. Humans are omnivores. We eat a variety of foods that require both types of teeth. Pay attention the next time you eat. Which teeth do you use to eat which foods?

Chewing food is important to the digestive process. When teeth break down the food into smaller pieces, it is easier for the digestive juices to begin their job of reacting with the food. Also, saliva can mix with the small bits of food easier, beginning to break down **starches** into sugars.

On the Tip of Your Tongue

Your tongue also aids the digestion process. It moves the food to the grinding teeth and assists with the mashing. It also helps make the food into a glob called a *bolus*. The tongue then moves the bolus to the back of the throat so you can swallow it.

Slippery Saliva

Meanwhile, your salivary **glands** are busy squirting saliva into your mouth. This liquid wets the food. Saliva is 99 percent water, so when someone says that his "mouth is watering," he isn't too far from the truth.

Saliva also begins breaking down the food. This makes the food mushy so you can swallow it. Amylase is one of the chemicals found in saliva. It turns complex **carbohydrates**, or starches, into sugars.

Experts say your salivary glands make two or more cups of saliva every day. That's a lot of spit!

Try This!

Chew an unsalted cracker until it tastes sweet. The trick is to keep chewing and not swallow. If you hold the cracker in your mouth long enough, it will start to taste sweet. Why?

Thanks to the amylase in your saliva, some of the starch in the cracker has turned into a sugar. Unlike starches, sugars can slip through your small intestine walls into the blood vessels. Sugar **molecules** are also small enough to slip into your cells. In the cells, the sugar combines with oxygen. This chemical **reaction** gives off energy the body can use.

Down the Food Pipe to the Stomach

The Esophagus

Gather some saliva in your mouth and swallow it. Use a clock to time seven to ten seconds from the moment you swallowed. That's how long it took for the saliva to reach your stomach. Food takes the same amount of time to travel to your stomach.

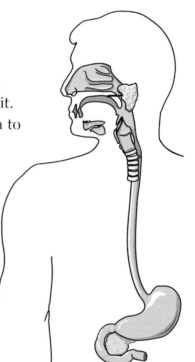

Now swallow again, but this time place your fingers on the front of your throat. Did you feel your Adam's apple? It's the bump in the middle of your throat. Did you feel it go up and down when you swallowed? Have you ever thought about why it does that? Is it a food elevator delivering the goods to your stomach? No. Actually, the Adam's apple is your larynx, or voice box, which helps you speak. It has nothing to do with digestion.

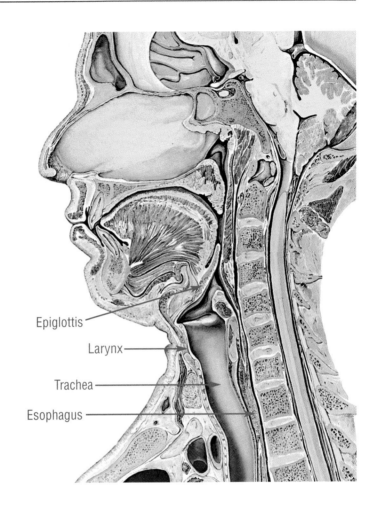

Epiglottis

Larynx

Trachea

Esophagus

However, the larynx does move up to press against a flap called the *epiglottis* each time you swallow. The epiglottis then closes off the trachea, or windpipe. This flap keeps food from going down the wrong pipe into your lungs. Try breathing while swallowing. You won't be able to do it since both tubes can't be open at the same time.

The esophagus, your food pipe, is right behind the windpipe. Food and saliva pass to the stomach through the esophagus.

What moves your swallowed food down to the stomach? Gravity may seem like the obvious answer, but there's more to it than that. Eat something bent over so that your head is lower than your stomach. (A talented person can try this while standing on her head!) You will find that swallowing works just as well in that position. That's because the muscles of your esophagus squeeze and push the food toward the stomach. This squeezing muscle action is called *peristalsis*.

You can imagine the muscles pushing the food down if you picture a small ball being squeezed through a long sock or a sweater sleeve. Or imagine squeezing toothpaste out of a tube. Both actions are similar to what the esophagus does to push food along.

The Stomach

Have you ever had a gurgling, rumbling stomach? Has a burp slipped out when you least wanted it to? It's okay. It's just your digestive system letting you know that it's hard at work for you.

When the food reaches the bottom of the esophagus, it checks into the stomach hotel. Lots of people think the stomach is at waist level or below. Actually, it is above the waist, in between the lower ribs, just below the breastbone. Feel where your ribs meet in front. The bone that runs up and down between them is your breastbone. Your stomach is just below that. Its bottom is level with your bottom ribs.

How Do You Know When You're Hungry?

What lets you know that you're hungry? Is it your rumbling stomach or your nose that smells freshly baked chocolate chip cookies? No, it's actually a part of your brain called the *hypothalamus*. The hypothalamus controls your feelings of hunger. If your hypothalamus is damaged, you may feel hungry all the time or never feel hungry at all. If your stomach is damaged or even removed, however, you still feel hunger pains.

The stomach is a stretchy, muscular sack. Some stomachs are shaped like a half moon. Others have a shape similar to the letters S or J. The shape of your stomach doesn't affect digestion.

An adult's stomach holds $1\frac{1}{2}$ to 2 quarts of food and liquid. Powerful stomach walls squeeze and mash the food. Hunger pains or a gurgling stomach happen if the stomach kneads when it's empty.

The stomach also breaks up food with digestive juices. One of those juices is hydrochloric acid. Hydrochloric acid from the stomach is strong enough to eat a hole in a rug. It would eat holes in your stomach too except that the stomach has a protective coating.

Try This!

Pour $1\frac{1}{2}$ to 2 quarts of water into a plastic bag. This will give you an idea of how big the stomach is and how much it holds.

What marvelous stuff saves your stomach from this powerful acid? Mighty mucus does. In fact, mucus coats most of your digestive tract. This slimy substance protects your stomach and helps your food slide right along.

Stomachs have the ability to stretch or shrink as needed. You may have noticed your stomach sticking out after you made a pig of yourself at the dinner table. Sometimes the carbon dioxide gas that is **dissolved** in sodas to make them bubbly **expands** in your stomach. Then you have to burp to let the gas out. Some foods can also produce gases that make you burp.

Your food stays in the stomach for a few hours, interacting with digestive juices. When the stomach has finished its job, the food has become a runny mush called *chyme*. When it is watery enough, chyme gets squirted out a bit at a time through an opening in the lower stomach. Your food, or what's left of it, has now checked out of the stomach hotel.

Stomach Juices

Digestive juices in the stomach are also called *gastric juices*. So remember, stomach=gas=gastric!

Try This!

Cut off the bottom of a paper cup and use it like a stethoscope to listen to a partner's stomach. Try this right before or after a meal if possible. The stomach noises you hear before a meal are most likely the sounds of the stomach muscles pushing air around in the stomach. Right after a meal, the sounds are the churning or mashing of the food with the digestive juices.

CHAPTER 3

Introducing the Intestines

When the chyme leaves the stomach, it drops into the small intestine. Eventually it makes its way to the large intestine. The two intestines are found in the **abdomen**, below the belly button.

The Small Intestine

The small intestine is smaller around than the large intestine. It is about $1\frac{1}{2}$ to 2 inches around—as big as a quarter or a garden hose.

Small intestine

The small intestine is a great deal longer than the large intestine. In a grown-up, the small intestine is about 20 feet long. It looks like a looped and coiled muscular hose.

Most of your food gets digested in the small intestine. Muscles there squeeze and push the food along slowly. The food moves about three inches a minute. This slow pace gives the digestive process plenty of time to work.

Digestive juices from the small intestine team up with juices from the liver, pancreas, and gallbladder to attack the chyme. They work together to finish changing the food into nutrients the body can use. Your food has now been through a complete makeover. It has changed into completely different substances that can now enter the bloodstream and be used as fuel or as building blocks by your body.

The inside walls of the small intestines are lined with about five million tiny villi. Villi are finger-shaped bumps less than a millimeter long. As many as 4000 of them could fit in a spot the size of your fingernail.

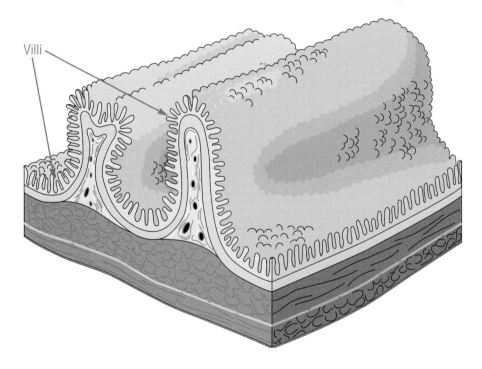

Villi

Villi stick out into the food passing by them and soak up the nutrients. Nutrients pass through thin villi walls and into the capillaries inside. Capillaries are tiny blood vessels. Once the nutrients get into the capillaries, blood carries them to other parts of the body.

The Large Intestine

The food that makes it through the small intestine goes on to the large intestine. The large intestine is bigger around than the small intestine but much shorter. It is about 3 to 4 inches around and 5 feet long in an adult. It also curves around tightly to fit in a small space in your abdomen.

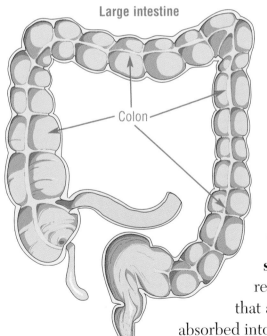

Large intestine

Colon

The majority of the large intestine is called the *colon*. The colon absorbs water, minerals, and **body salts** from the undigested food. The parts of the food that are not usable get pushed along. The large intestine acts as a water recycler and trash compactor for the body.

After getting compacted, or pushed together tightly, the brownish leftovers are **semisolid**. Most of the remaining water and any minerals that are left at this point are absorbed into the bloodstream in the colon.

Inside your large intestine are millions of "friendly" bacteria. These bacteria are helpful to your body. These tiny living things help break down plant material in your food. They also help process **bile**. They even make vitamin K for you, which helps protect your heart and bones. In addition, these "good" bacteria help your body get nutrients from your food. There are enough of these friendly bacteria in the large intestine to almost fill a cup.

Why Is It There?

Attached to the large intestine is your tiny wormlike appendix. The appendix is part of the digestive path, but we don't seem to use this body part for digestion. It is believed that our ancestors may have needed it to help break down **fibers** in their leafy diet. Some scientists believe that today our bodies may use the appendix as part of the **immune system**.

An **inflamed** appendix is called *appendicitis*. When this happens, a surgeon will remove your appendix.

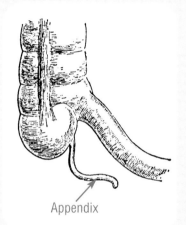

Appendix

A Long Journey

The total length of the small and large intestines of an adult is about 25 feet. Think of how tall that would make you if it were stretched out straight from end to end! Instead, the intestines are tightly coiled and wound up to take up only a small space in your abdomen.

If an adult's whole alimentary canal were pulled straight (ouch!), it would be as long as a school bus. The long length gives your body time to break down food and absorb nutrients.

The End of the Journey

Once all of the nutrients have been removed from your food, the waste, or feces, is stored in the rectum until you go to the bathroom. The rectum is at the bottom end of the large intestine. The waste passes out the anus, a small hole at the bottom of your rectum. This waste contains food you couldn't digest, digestive juices, and dead bacteria. About 18 to 30 hours after you eat, the food you ate has completed its journey through the digestive system.

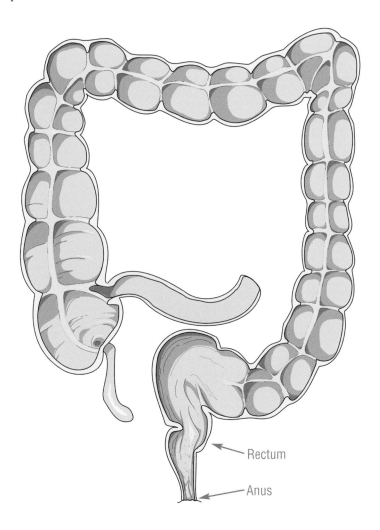

Rectum

Anus

CHAPTER 4

Helping Out: The Liver, Pancreas, and Gallbladder

The liver, pancreas, and gallbladder are not part of the alimentary canal. Food does not pass through them. But they are part of the digestive system because they contribute digestive juices to break down your food.

The Liver

The liver is your largest internal, or inside, organ. An adult's liver weighs about 3⅓ pounds. This soft, reddish-brown organ sits on the right side of the upper abdomen, just below the ribs.

The liver is one very busy organ. It performs over 600 jobs for your body. About 1½ quarts of blood flow through it every minute. Blood flows to the liver straight from the heart and intestines. The blood coming from the intestines is carrying dissolved nutrients to the liver. The liver then processes them for the whole body.

The liver also controls the amount of sugar in your blood. It manages the levels of vitamins, minerals, fats, and sugars in the blood by storing them until they are needed. It also takes iron from broken-down red blood cells and stores it until it is needed for new blood cells.

Toxins, germs, and drugs are filtered through the liver to keep the body safe. People can damage their livers by drinking too much alcohol or taking harmful drugs.

The liver makes over a quart of bile every day for digesting fats. Bile is a yellow or greenish liquid that helps break down and absorb fats. Because the fats that you eat form large **globules**, they must be broken up into smaller pieces to be digested. Bile breaks up these fat globules so that **enzymes** can surround them and break them up even more in the small intestine.

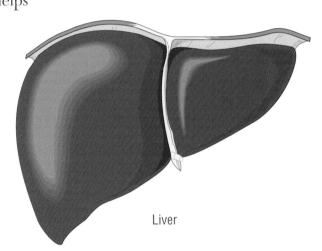

Liver

Try This!

Dish detergent is a lot like bile. Dish soap breaks up fats in dishwater similar to how bile does in the intestine.

Pour some oil into a small jar or bottle. Add water and dish detergent. Shake it up. What do you notice?

You should see the oil broken up into tiny droplets. Picture bile doing this to fats in your small intestine.

The Pancreas

The pancreas is about six inches long. This pinkish organ is shaped a little like a bumpy, wavy carrot. It sits just beneath the stomach.

The pancreas makes pancreatic juice, which breaks down starches, **proteins**, and fats. Your pancreas makes about $1\frac{1}{2}$ quarts of this important digestive juice each day. The enzymes in pancreatic juice digest proteins, carbohydrates, and fats, which are three major nutrients. Pancreatic juice also contains sodium bicarbonate. This substance helps lessen the burning effects of the stomach acid that is mixed in with the food that enters the intestine. Pancreatic juice flows along the pancreatic duct into the small intestine, where it helps digest the food.

Stomach

Pancreatic duct

Pancreas

The Gallbladder

The soft, stretchy gallbladder is tucked behind the liver. This small organ stores bile from the liver. The gallbladder can store up to $1\frac{1}{2}$ ounces of bile at a time. When bile is needed to help break down food, it is released into the small intestine through the bile duct.

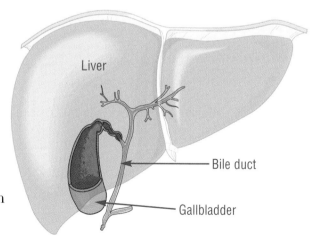

Liver

Bile duct

Gallbladder

CHAPTER 5

Teaming Up with Nutrition

The main job of the digestive system is to absorb the nutrients you need from your food. The more nutrients you take in, the healthier you will be. Nutrients also provide the energy you need to think, move, and grow.

Food Is Fuel for Your Body

All movement requires energy. A car's energy comes from its fuel—gasoline. Gasoline is burned in the car's engine to release energy. Your body's fuel is its food. It gets "burned" in your cells.

Like a car, you need a continuous supply of energy. Everything you do requires energy. The more active you are, the more energy you burn. Playing football and basketball will burn more energy than sitting in front of the TV. However, just sitting around watching TV does take some energy. Even sleeping uses energy.

Your body is busy inside even if it doesn't look busy outside. Thinking takes energy. The brain uses a lot of fuel. Your heart beating and your lungs breathing take energy. All of your body's cells use energy to do their jobs. Even digesting food to get energy takes energy.

You also burn a lot of fuel keeping your body warm inside. **Cold-blooded** animals like reptiles, fish, and amphibians don't need to eat as much or as often as **warm-blooded** animals like humans do. You need more energy to maintain your warm body temperature.

You need six kinds of nutrients. These are carbohydrates, proteins, fats, vitamins, minerals, and water. Good nutrition means eating healthy foods so that your body gets the right amount of these important nutrients. The best thing you can do for your digestive system is give it lots of these six sources of nutrients.

Lizards are cold-blooded reptiles. They use heat energy from the Sun to warm themselves.

Carbohydrates

Carbohydrates supply your body with much of the energy it needs. The digestive system turns carbohydrates into blood glucose (blood sugar), which is a main source of fuel for the body. It is the only source of energy for the brain.

Carbohydrates are found in foods that come from plants, such as vegetables, fruits, and grains. Milk and other dairy products are the only foods from animals that are also a good source of carbohydrates.

Carbohydrates are divided into two groups—simple and complex. Simple carbohydrates are sugars. Sugars include fructose (the sugar found in fruit), lactose (the sugar found in milk), sucrose (table sugar), and other sugars. Fruits are a rich source of simple carbohydrates.

Complex carbohydrates are starches. Peas, beans, and potatoes are vegetables that contain starch. Foods made from grains like corn, oats, rice, and wheat are also good sources of starch. Breads, cereals, and pastas are made from these grains.

Try This!

Test foods for starch. Gather a variety of food samples. Mix a small amount of iodine with water until it is a light brown color. Put drops of the mixture on the food samples. If the iodine mixture turns dark blue to black when it touches the food, there is starch in the food.

Make a chart showing which foods contained starch and which did not. Were there any surprises?

Proteins

Proteins are needed for growth, repair, and replacement of cells. They help build muscles and organs as you grow. If you scrape a knee, protein helps repair the skin and make new skin cells. Proteins are mainly found in meats, fish, eggs, nuts, and beans. They can also be found in dairy products, such as milk, cheese, and yogurt.

Fats

Although fat is often seen as a bad thing, the body actually needs some of this important nutrient. During the first two years of life, a baby needs a larger amount of fat for normal brain development. After about age two, though, only a small amount of fat is necessary. The key is to get enough fat, but not too much.

Fats are a part of all body cells. They provide padding for organs like the heart and lungs. They also help keep the body warm by **insulating** it from cold.

Fats are a good source of energy. They help absorb certain vitamins the body needs.

Fats are found in meats, oils, and egg yolks. Dairy products such as margarine, cream, butter, cheese, ice cream, and nonskim milk also contain fat.

Vitamins and Minerals

When you were a child, did you take chewable vitamins in the shape of Scooby-Doo or the Flintstones? Perhaps you still take vitamins today. This is because vitamins and minerals are very important nutrients that all people need to stay healthy. Vitamins and minerals are found naturally in foods such as fruits, vegetables, and meats. They have also been added to many packaged foods such as cereals and breads.

Vitamins help you fight germs and keep your body running smoothly. They help the body grow. Each vitamin has its own job, but many of them work together to keep your body healthy.

> ### Try This!
>
> Test foods for fat. Cut a brown paper bag into squares. Gather some foods to test. Predict which ones will be fatty.
>
> To test for fat, rub or press the food on the paper until it makes a spot. If the food is a liquid, place a few drops on the paper. Label each spot with the name of the food. Set the paper aside to dry. After the paper dries, check to see which spots still look wet. Those foods contain fat. The larger the fat spot, the more fat in the food.
>
> Compare your results to your predictions. How many did you get right?

Bananas are a rich source of vitamin B6 and the mineral potassium.

Vitamin A is found in green and yellow fruits and vegetables. Fish oils also contain this vitamin. Vitamin A is needed for healthy skin, strong bones, and good vision. It also helps fight **infections** in the body.

The B vitamins help the body digest proteins, carbohydrates, and fats. The nervous system and red blood cells depend on these vitamins. The B vitamins also contribute to healthy teeth, gums, skin, and hair. Meats, seafoods, leafy vegetables, dairy products, eggs, and grains are good sources of these vitamins.

Vitamin C is found in berries, citrus fruits, and green vegetables. Vitamin C is needed for tissue growth and repair. It also helps fight illness and disease.

Fish, dairy products, and eggs contain vitamin D. This vitamin creates strong bones and teeth. Your body can make its own vitamin D when you get enough sunlight.

Minerals work with vitamins to build strong bodies. You need minerals to live, but you cannot produce them in your body. It is very important, therefore, to eat the right foods to get enough minerals.

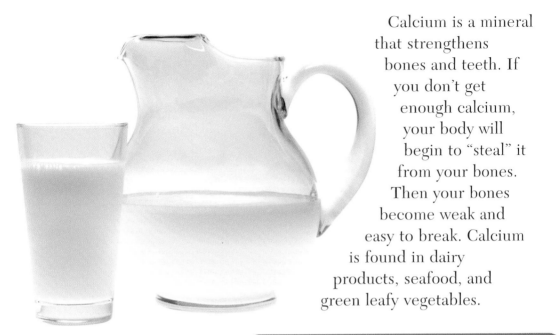

Calcium is a mineral that strengthens bones and teeth. If you don't get enough calcium, your body will begin to "steal" it from your bones. Then your bones become weak and easy to break. Calcium is found in dairy products, seafood, and green leafy vegetables.

Iron is important for the blood. It helps blood carry oxygen to all parts of your body. Not getting enough iron can make you tired and crabby. This mineral is found in eggs, fish, red meats, green leafy vegetables, beans, peas, and grain products.

Try This!

Minerals are important to your health. How many can you name? Check out the list of common minerals below to see how many you recognize.

boron	phosphorus
calcium	potassium
chromium	selenium
copper	sodium
iodine	sulfur
iron	zinc
magnesium	

Find out more about these minerals. Do you get enough of them in your diet? What do they do for your body? What foods should you eat to get them? Share your information with your friends and family.

Water

Your body is about 70 percent water. This water is involved in every function of the body. Blood, which is mostly water, carries nutrients around your body. It also helps carry waste out of your cells. Some vitamins need water to help them dissolve into a usable form. Water helps keep your body from becoming too hot or cold inside.

Moisture is important to the body. Your body can't live more than a few days without a fresh supply of water. You lose water every day through **urination**, sweat, etc.

Try This!

Find a scale that can weigh small things in grams or ounces. Weigh a sliced apple and a peeled carrot. Record the weights. Leave the items alone for a few days until they look shriveled up. Weigh them again. What is the difference in the weights?

The difference in weight equals the water that **evaporated** from the food. Were you surprised at how much water the foods contained?

You can try this experiment with just about any fresh fruit or vegetable. Just make sure you cut or peel them so they can dry out.

It is important to balance this loss by taking in as much water as you lose. If you get too dried out, or dehydrated, you can become ill or die.

Drinking lots of water each day will keep your body in good condition. You can also get water from many of the foods you eat. Most fruits and vegetables contain large amounts of water.

Try This!

If you want to get a rough idea of how many gallons of water your body has, you can figure it out by weight. Multiply your weight by .70. That will tell you about how much of your weight is water.

There are 8.34 pounds of water in 1 gallon. Divide your water weight by 8.34 to find the approximate number of gallons of water in your body.

Example based on a 100-pound person:
100 pounds x .70 = 70 pounds
70 pounds ÷ 8.34 = 8.4 gallons
So a 100-pound body has 70 pounds, or 8.4 gallons, of water.

What Should You Be Digesting?

Your health and your digestion depend on the foods you eat. To be healthy, you should eat a balance of all the nutrients each day. You should also limit the amount of snack foods and fast food you eat.

Ever notice that you get a stomachache after eating a huge hamburger and salty pile of fries? That's because healthy foods are easier to digest than fatty or greasy foods. Eating lots of junk food is hard on your digestive system and doesn't provide you with the nutrients your body needs.

Pick from the Pyramid

To help people choose foods that provide the necessary nutrients, the U.S. government developed the Food Guide Pyramid. This food pyramid helps you choose a healthy diet.

You should eat the most of the foods at the bottom of the pyramid. Six to eleven servings from the bread, cereal, rice, and pasta group each day will provide necessary carbohydrates and other nutrients.

Fats, oils, and sweets
Use sparingly

Milk, yogurt, and cheese
2–3 Servings

Protein (meat, fish, eggs, beans, nuts)
2–3 Servings

Vegetables
3–5 Servings

Fruits
2–4 Servings

Grains (bread, cereal, rice, pasta)
6–11 Servings

Given the choice between broccoli and potato chips or an apple or a cookie, which would you choose? Unfortunately, many people would choose the chips and the cookie. Most people have trouble eating enough foods out of the next groups on the pyramid—the fruit and vegetable groups. You should have three to five servings of vegetables and two to four servings of fruit every day. Fruits and vegetables are a big source of many important vitamins and minerals.

Two or three servings from the milk, yogurt, and cheese group are recommended. Much of your daily calcium and vitamin D needs are met by this group.

The meat, poultry, fish, dry beans, eggs, and nuts group is your main source of iron and protein. Two or three servings a day from this group are a smart choice.

Serving Sizes

Ever wonder how much of a food makes up a serving? Here are a few examples from each group.

bread, cereal, rice, and pasta group
1 slice of bread
1 cup of cold cereal
$1/2$ cup of cooked cereal, rice,
  or pasta

vegetable group
1 cup of salad
$1/2$ cup of other
  vegetables

fruit group
1 apple, banana, or orange
$1/2$ cup of other fruits
$3/4$ cup of fruit juice

milk, yogurt, and cheese group
1 cup of yogurt or milk
$1^1/2$ to 2 ounces of cheese (an ounce is about the size of a 1-inch cube)

meat, poultry, fish, dry beans, eggs, and nuts group
2 to 3 ounces of meat, poultry, or fish (about the size of a deck of cards)
4 to 6 tablespoons of peanut butter
1 egg
$1/2$ cup of cooked beans

Nutrition Facts

Serving Size 1/4 package (25g)
Servings Per Container 4

Amount Per Serving	As Packaged	1/2 cup Prepared with 2% Lowfat Milk
Calories	90	150
Calories from Fat	0	20

	% Daily Value**	
Total Fat 0g*	0%	4%
Saturated Fat 0g	0%	7%
Cholesterol 0mg	0%	3%
Sodium 390mg	16%	19%
Total Carbohydrate 23g	8%	10%
Dietary Fiber 0g	0%	0%
Sugars 18g		
Protein 0g		
Vitamin A	0%	4%
Vitamin C	0%	0%
Calcium	0%	15%
Iron	0%	0%

* Amount in dry mix
** Percent Daily Values are based on a 2,000 calorie diet.

INGREDIENTS: SUGAR, DEXTROSE (FROM CORN), MODIFIED FOOD STARCH, DISODIUM PHOSPHATE AND TETRA SODIUM PYROPHOSPH... THICKENING), CONTAI... 2% OF NATURAL FLAV... FLAVOR, SALT, MONO... ERIDES (PREVENT FOA... COLOR, YELLOW 6, YEL... COLOR, BUTTER, BHA...

PIE DIRECT...
1. **PREPARE**
   directed fo...
   reducing m...
   1 3/4 cups...
   pie, use 2 ...
   (4-serving ...
   3 1/2 cups...
2. **POUR** at o...
   9-inch cru...
   baked past...
   cooled.
3. **REFRIGER...**
   least 1 hou...
   (3 hours for fuller
   pie) or until set.

Try This!

Be aware of what you eat. Check out the nutrition labels. Choose five foods and compare their nutritional facts. Which have more fat? sugar? nutrients? calories? Make a chart of your findings.

Were you surprised? Not all foods are as healthy as they appear. Some sweetened cereals have more sugar in them than a candy bar.

The foods on the top of the pyramid should only be eaten once in a while. This is the fats, oils, and sweets section. The pyramid does not give a serving size for these foods since you don't need to eat them for nutrition. You should eat these foods "sparingly," which means in small amounts. Fried foods, candy, cakes, donuts, whipped cream, sour cream, butter, mayonnaise, salad dressings, sodas, milkshakes, ice cream, and chips all fit into this group. These foods may taste great, but they don't provide enough nutrition to be worth the grease, fat, sugar, and high calories.

Fiber Facts

Another thing to be aware of when making healthy choices is the amount of fiber you're eating. Fiber is a part of a plant that resists digestion. Only a small amount of fiber is digested by your body. Most of it moves through your digestive tract and ends up as waste.

How does this help digestion? Fiber holds on to water, which is good for digestion. Because fiber stays in your digestive tract, it builds up quickly. The overload of fiber forces your body to empty waste faster. This keeps your digestive tract clean.

Fiber is found in foods that come from plants, such as fruits, vegetables, and grain products. Eating lots of these foods will help keep your digestive system healthy.

Energy: Take In What You Burn Up

The amount of energy in foods is measured in calories. The number of calories you take in each day should equal the amount of energy you use up. If you digest more calories than you burn, you'll gain weight. If you burn more calories than you digest, you'll lose weight.

The number of calories you need each day depends on several things. Your age, whether you are a boy or girl, your height and weight, and how active you are all affect how much energy you burn. A 10- to 12-year-old girl needs about 2200 to 2300 calories per day. A 10- to 12-year-old boy needs around 2400 to 2500 calories. If you are active, you burn more calories. If you are a couch potato, you burn fewer. To keep a healthy weight, balance the calories you take in with the calories you burn up.

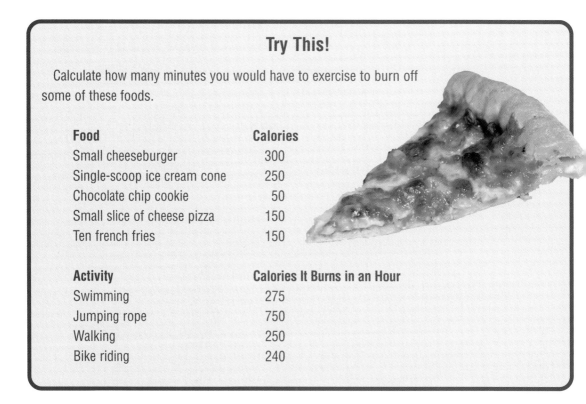

Try This!

Calculate how many minutes you would have to exercise to burn off some of these foods.

Food	Calories
Small cheeseburger	300
Single-scoop ice cream cone	250
Chocolate chip cookie	50
Small slice of cheese pizza	150
Ten french fries	150

Activity	Calories It Burns in an Hour
Swimming	275
Jumping rope	750
Walking	250
Bike riding	240

Start Off Right

Eating breakfast every day will improve your health and digestion. When you eat a healthy breakfast, it gets your digestive system going. Your body will start to absorb the nutrients it needs for the day. Your brain power and energy will increase, so eating breakfast will also help you do better in school.

Get Moving!

Besides eating healthy, exercise also aids your digestion. Physical activity keeps food moving through the colon. It also helps burn calories to balance the energy you digest and the energy you use.

Conclusion

The old saying "you are what you eat" has a lot of truth to it. What you put into your body affects how you think, how you move, and how you feel. Feed yourself nutritious foods, and your digestive system will reward you with strength and energy. Give your body the nutrients it needs, and it will pay you back for many years to come.

The digestive system is just one player on an awesome team of body systems. Your digestive system works tirelessly to take in food and transform it into fuel for your body. It delivers building materials to your cells so the body can grow and repair itself. It carries water to refresh all of your systems. It even gets rid of waste that your body doesn't need.

This powerful system works closely with other body systems. The respiratory system brings in oxygen so the cells can "burn" food for energy. The circulatory system delivers nutrients and oxygen to all the body's cells. It also hauls away waste products from these cells. The brain and nervous system run the whole show with help from your senses.

This dynamic team is a definite winner, but it needs your support. Feed it healthy foods so that it can get the carbohydrates, proteins, fats, vitamins, and minerals it needs. Drink plenty of water. Exercise to keep your systems moving. With your help, you and your body will be champions!

Internet Connections and Related Reading for the Digestive System

http://www.kidshealth.org/kid/body/digest_noSW.html
Get "The Real Deal on the Digestive System" from this Kids Health site.

http://yucky.kids.discovery.com/noflash/body/pg000126.html
Discover the amazing journey your food takes through your digestive system.

http://www.innerbody.com/image/digeov.html
Click on the parts of the digestive system for information on each one. This site also includes an overview of the entire system.

http://vilenski.org/science/humanbody/hb_html/digestivesystem.html
Check out this diagram of the digestive system along with some interesting facts. You can also take an up-close look at the liver and gallbladder.

http://library.thinkquest.org/10348/find/content/
digestive.html?tqskip1=1&tqtime=1118
Learn some basic information about the digestive journey, view diagrams of the digestive organs, and take a quiz to see how much you've learned.

http://www.kidshealth.org/kid/stay_healthy/food/pyramid.html
This site introduces kids to the food pyramid, nutrients, and vitamins and minerals.

http://www.howstuffworks.com/food.htm
Find out how food works. How is it digested and changed into energy your body needs? Learn about the seven important materials (six nutrients plus fiber) you must feed your body to stay healthy.

Digestion by Steve Parker. Offers students a comprehensive picture of digestion. Millbrook Press, 1997. [RL 5 IL 4–6] (3111006 HB)

Human Body by Steve Parker. An Eyewitness Book on the human body. Dorling Kindersley, 1993. [RL 7.7 IL 3–8] (5868906 HB)

The Magic School Bus Inside the Human Body by Joanna Cole. Welcome aboard the Magic School Bus for a close-up look at how human bodies get energy from food. Scholastic, 1989. [RL 3 IL 3–6] (4297901 PB 4297902 CC)

What Happens to a Hamburger by Paul Showers. This guided tour of the digestive system is an appealing and informative introduction to the fascinating process of digestion. HarperCollins, 1985. [RL 3 IL K–5] (8453301 PB 8453302 CC)

•RL = Reading Level
•IL = Interest Level
Perfection Learning's catalog numbers are included for your ordering convenience. PB indicates paperback. CC indicates Cover Craft. HB indicates hardback.

Glossary

abdomen (AB duh muhn) middle section of the body between the chest and the hips where the digestive organs lie (see separate entry for *organ*)

bile (beyel) substance made in the liver that helps digest fats

bloodstream (BLUHD streem) flow of blood throughout the body

body salt (BAH dee sawlt) material, including table salt and similar substances, used to help move water and nutrients through the colon

carbohydrate (kar boh HEYE drayt) material that comes from plants and is present in foods made from these plants, such as wheat and oats

cell (sel) smallest unit of living matter

chemical (KEM uh kuhl) substance produced by a scientific reaction (see separate entry for *reaction*)

circulatory system (SER kyuh luh tor ee SIS tuhm) system with the heart, blood, and blood vessels that carry blood to all parts of the body

cold-blooded (cohld BLUH ded) having a body temperature that changes with the temperature of the environment

dissolve (diz ZAHLV) combine with a liquid

enzyme (EN zeyem) substance produced by living cells that helps chemical reactions occur (see separate entries for *cell*, *chemical*, and *reaction*)

evaporate (ee VAP or ay ted) change from a liquid to a gas

expand (ik SPAND) spread out

fiber (FEYE ber) part of a plant that resists digestion

gland (gland) part of the body that secretes, or sends out, materials in the body

globule (GLAH byoul) tiny ball of liquid

immune system (im MYOUN SIS tuhm) parts of the body that attack germs and diseases

infection (in FEK shuhn) disease or illness in the body

inflamed (in FLAYMD) marked by warmth, redness, swelling, and/or pain

insulating (IN suh lay ting) preventing hot or cold from passing through

intestinal (in TES tin uhl) relating to the intestines, the tubes where food is broken down

molecule (MAHL uh kyoul) tiny bit, or particle, of a substance

mucus (MYOU kuhs) slippery substance in the body that moistens and protects

organ (OR guhn) body part that performs a specific job

protein (PROH teen) material found in plant and animal foods that helps cells grow (see separate entry for *cell*)

reaction (ree AK shuhn) response or change that occurs when two or more substances are mixed

semisolid (SEM ee sah lid) having the qualities of both a solid and a liquid; a mushy, runny solid

starch (starch) main form of complex carbohydrates in plants (see separate entry for *carbohydrate*)

toxin (TAHKS sin) poisonous substance

urination (yoor uh NAY shuhn) process of removing liquid waste from the body

warm-blooded (warm BLUH ded) having a constant warm body temperature that doesn't depend on the environment

Index